Singing Waters

Singing Waters

A Selection of
Haiku, Senryu,
and
Haibun

by Johnette Downing

🌢

Edited by
Stanford M. Forrester/*sekiro*

buddha baby press
windsor, connecticut

Singing Waters: A Selection of Haiku, Senryu, and Haibun
© 2022 by Johnette Downing ☯

Edited by Stanford M. Forrester/*sekiro*

Cover and book design
© 2022 Stanford M. Forrester/*sekiro*

ISBN: 978-1-7366037-5-8

Printed & published in the USA.

First On-Demand Edition, 2022 (Year of the Tiger)

For classroom or multiple copy discounts,
please contact the publisher.

buddha baby press is a service imprint of bottle rockets press

buddha baby press div.
bottle rockets press
P.O. Box 189
Windsor, Connecticut 06095, USA
www.bottlerocketspress.com
bottlerockets_99@yahoo.com

*With the deepest gratitude
to Thom Bennett
for introducing me to haiku.*

When you do things from your soul,
you feel a river moving in you,
a joy.

— Rumi

Introduction

I was introduced to haiku several decades ago when I received as a gift the book *Classic Haiku — A Master's Selection,* selected and translated by Yuzuru Miura, to read during a summer vacation in a log cabin positioned over a singing creek in the Western North Carolina mountains. My favorite poem in the book by Yosa Buson is a meditation about the sound of a temple bell.

After reading the book, I jumped into Bashō's frog pond with both feet, and have enjoyed the swim ever since. I was not taught the 5-7-5 grade school method of counting syllables; therefore, I adopted the modern Western approach to haiku which I define as: *a short, unrhymed, one breath poem of Japanese origin consisting of 17 syllables or fewer, written in three lines or fewer, with two concrete images separated by a pause in juxtaposition relating nature to human nature.* Ah, one breath, my kind of poetry! The description is longer than the poem.

I have lived my entire life near water, and naturally, as a musician, I hear music in water. There is music in haiku as well; therefore, I have divided this book into water chapters to evoke a mood even though few poems are about water. I hope you enjoy the score.

♦

Rain

dishwater sky
we walk through
the rinse cycle

roofers next door
their shadows
work on my house

he loves me not
she adds another petal
to the chalk flower

on the clothesline
a butterfly
dries its wings

half rainbow —
even the colors have run out
to play

the moon party
quiet
another cloud

she refuses
his kiss
neon moon

sky writing
his *I love you*
fades away

hole in the cloud
my nephew calls
for more money

nails _____

_____ chalkboard _____

_____ chills

a double-dog dare
sourball
candy

bubbles
from the fountain
goldfish eyes

Easter rain
the garden
resurrected

Pond

ripples in the pond
my mother's face
in mine

origami frog
with each tap
of the finger

evening fog
the sky
in my hand

releasing the dead plant
from its pot
wiggle of an earth worm

metamorphosis —
a butterfly flies
out of my shadow

Zen garden
a single
chime

katydid
katydidn't
insect gossip

edible flowers
the caterpillar
and I

Sunday morning
the gospel
according to birds

buttercups
a child's
yellow nose

sneaking past the old dog
unnoticed . . .
                    the old cat

Sunday morning
hymnals
mowers

wild daisies
all the times
I was wrong

Bayou

♦

dark bayou
a fish jumps
through the moon

breathless heat
her B&B
a Bible and Breakfast

winter chill
a love song my father wrote
not to my mother

shell of a cicada
a song
sung out

winter kudzu
the fence sheds
its coat

dandelions
old ladies
under hairdryers

7 Breaths

cut cane
the sweetness
of her insult

pine needles
daddy does
her hair

voodoo
an anti-theft
chicken foot

used bookstore
the cat
a rescue

aqua marine
salon
mishap

mosquitoes
and high water
all that is left

through the wall
their argument —
I take sides

fuchsia azaleas
playtime
in mother's makeup

first teen dance
first time she doesn't wave
first

email dating
she tries to sound
pretty

agapanthus
starched ladies
under umbrellas

family reunion
I return
to the girl I was

Mother

thinness
her eyelids
as I close them

I move her jaw
to close her mouth
the coolness

drip from the faucet
mother's words
in my mouth

grape leaves
her hands as I fold them
across her chest

Lake

migrating birds
taking the lake
with them

cold night
one cup
of tea

                                    r
                                        e
          March winds   v
          his   o
          c   o   m   b

pushing the clouds
away
my oar

cormorant
fishing
for himself

Morse code
stop
birds on a line

long walk
I replay the argument in my mind
until I've won

t
r
e
from the felled tree another

carrying the sun
away
fireflies

pink tutus
fluttering in the wind
spring butterflies

moon glow
each turning
of the page

final inning
the crowd
finds religion

snow in the bend of a branch
I let him
be right

so quiet
I hear his apology
coming

old church bell
flutter of birds
on the hour

moving day
we leave behind memories
less dear

thrift store
second hand
smoke

tea leaves
I turn the cup this way
that way

I pause
the audio book
mountain valley lake

River

dawn on the sand bar
the river's new
shape

polka dots
farther apart
at the hips

roller coaster
leaving my voice
at the top

river sunset
lemon slice sinking
in iced tea

he kisses
the moons
from her eyes

walking the labyrinth
the switchback path
of the ant

lunch box
her doll
a stowaway

wild mint
he gives in
a little

slice of moon
he says he likes
to miss me

freeing the mouse from the   trap

watching the crowd
eyes of the portrait
sitter

her dementia
I sort the stones
from the rice

under strands of Spanish moss
a novel
in Chinese

New Orleans

In my home of New Orleans, we celebrate everything, even funerals. During our celebrations, you are sure to find a second line. With origins in jazz funeral traditions, a second line is a parade of joyous people following a brass band up and down the streets of New Orleans to celebrate the passing of a loved one to a better place. The first line is the parade of silent mourners following the coffin to the grave. Handkerchiefs used in the first line to wipe tears are used in the second line to punctuate the beat of the music from a lively brass band.

coffin
in the curves
of the tuba

silk scarves
in the breeze
my ancestors

(continued on the next page . . .)

cemetery workers
digging
the music

Jesus sign
nailed to a
telephone pole

Hurricane Katrina

On August 29, 2005, Hurricane Katrina, a Category 5, barreled into coastal Louisiana, Mississippi, and Alabama packing winds of 175 mph, and a maximum storm surge of 28 ft. In New Orleans, levee failures caused floodwater to engulf 80% of the city, and did not recede for weeks. One million people were without power, and hundreds of thousands of people were forced into exile for months. The storm took the lives of approximately 1,833 people, and thousands of animals.

only the living
in the boat
his mother stays behind

flooding neighboring states
hurricane
evacuees

New Orleans moon
the color
of mud

(continued on the next page . . .)

tears of a stranger
leave their mark
on me

a shell
of what was
locust

marshland fly way
flying
away

a field of flowers
where the houses
were

dry riverbed
she moves on
with her life

Ocean

tide pool —
children
come and go

Moroccan sky
the clouds
in Arabic

magnolia blossom
I unfold the kimono
instructions

Nicaraguan night
I translate
the dog's bark

atop the Mayan temple
tourists
avoiding the sun

Chinese take-out
the cat waves
waves

gathering sea shells
one moves
in my pocket

tai chi class
the weight
of air

beaten to death
for candy

|

piñata

incense
her hair
out of the scarf

Beverly Hills Hilton
they assume
we're somebody

across the fish tank
a child's
eyes

withered chrysanthemum —
the warmth
of a tea cup

labyrinth
the first stone
the last

About the Poet

Recipient of the 2017 Louisiana Writer Award, Johnette Downing is a musician, author, illustrator, and haiku poet with twenty-eight books and eleven recordings. Cofounder of the former New Orleans Haiku Society, Johnette's haiku have appeared in *bottle rockets, Frogpond, Modern Haiku, Red Moon Anthologies,* and *World Haiku*, among others. Her poem "ripples in the pond" received a Haiku International Association Honorable Mention Award in Japan. She divides her time between New Orleans, Louisiana and Newburyport, Massachusetts. *Singing Waters* is her first book of haiku, senryu, and haibun.

Acknowledgments

I am grateful to the editors of the following publications in which many of these poems previously appeared: *bottle rockets: a collection of short verse,* Charlotte Digregorio's *Daily Haiku, Frogpond, Haiku International Association*, Haiku Society of America Member's Anthologies, *Magnolia 2 Press, Modern Haiku, New Orleans Haiku Society, Nisqually Delta Review, O' Muse Magazine, Pass It On!,* Press Here, Red Moon Press, Solaris Hill, The Haiku Foundation, Tiny Words, Trembling Pillow Press, World Haiku, and *YAWP*.

"ripples in the pond" received a Haiku International Association Honorable Mention Award in Japan.

Thank you to my husband Scott Billington for his love and support.

A special thank you and deep bow to Stanford M. Forrester *(sekiro)* for taking me under his wings, and helping me find my own.